Count-a-saurus

by Nancy Blumenthal
illustrated by Robert Jay Kaufman

HEINEMANN · LONDON

for

Jake and Ben

and for

Rebecca and Sara

Grateful acknowledgment to David D. Gillette, Ph.D., state palaeontologist of Utah, for his expert reading of this manuscript. And special thanks to Cindy Kane and Cecilia Yung.

William Heinemann Ltd
Michelin House
81 Fulham Road
London SW3 6RB

LONDON MELBOURNE AUCKLAND

First published in Great Britain in 1990
This edition published by arrangement with Four Winds Press, Macmillan Publishing Company, 866 Third Avenue, New York

ISBN 434 92878 X

Printed in Hong Kong

 One Stegosaurus standing in the sun.
(Steg-o-SOAR-us)

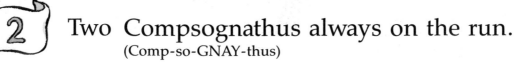 Two Compsognathus always on the run.
(Comp-so-GNAY-thus)

 Three Allosaurus gnashing pointy teeth.
(Al-o-SOAR-us)

 4 Four Iguanodon scratching itchy feet.
(Ig-WAN-o-don)

 5 Five Archaeopteryx gliding to a rock.
(Ar-kee-OP-tur-iks)

 6 Six Ceratopsians wearing frills and purple socks.
(Ser-a-TOP-see-ans)

 7 Seven Plesiosaurus swimming in the seas.
(Plee-zee-o-SOAR-us)

 Eight Brontosaurus browsing in the trees.
(Bron-toe-SOAR-us)

9 Nine Ankylosaurus with armour on their backs.
(Ann-kie-lo-SOAR-us)

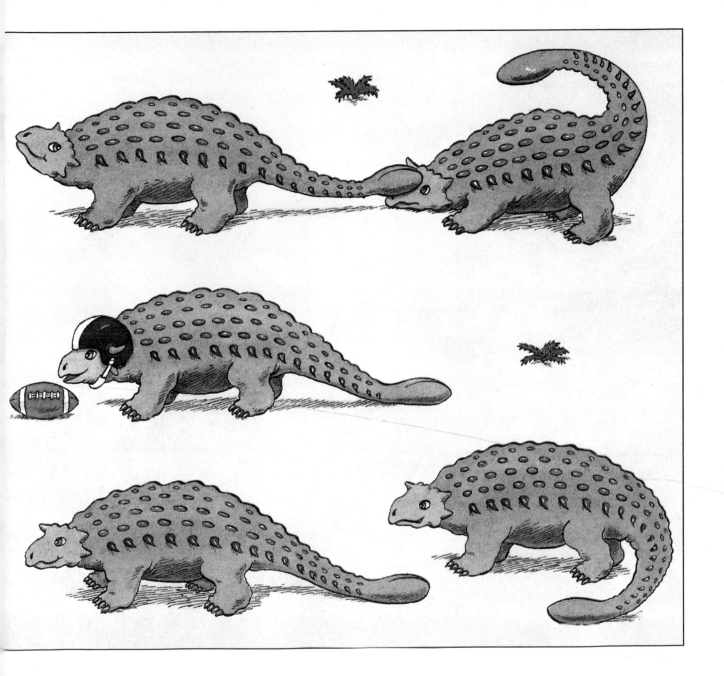

10 Ten Hadrosaurids sporting funny hats.
(Had-ro-SOAR-ids)

Now one to ten we sing the chorus....

This is how we count-a-saurus!

One Stegosaurus standing in the sun.

Why did Stegosaurus have those bony plates on its back? The sharp, angular plates might have helped Stegosaurus protect itself. Scientists also think the plates may have served as an early solar heating-cooling system for Stegosaurus. Those bony plates were full of tiny blood vessels. Standing sideways to the sun could have been Stegosaurus's method of warming up! When Stegosaurus got too warm it could change position and face directly into the sun. Then the rays would pass over the bony plates and this plant-eating dinosaur could cool off.

Two Compsognathus always on the run.

Compsognathus was one of the smallest dinosaurs. No bigger than a chicken, it had long, thin legs and was a speedy runner. A light frame enabled this carnivore, or meat-eater, to catch other fast-moving animals such as small lizards or dragonflies.

Three Allosaurus gnashing pointy teeth.

Allosaurus was another carnivorous dinosaur. Many of us think of the meat-eating dinosaurs as mean and ferocious. But it's important to remember they were just following their instincts. They attacked their prey in order to survive and only when they were hungry.

Four Iguanodon scratching itchy feet.

Did you notice the spiked thumbs on Iguanodon's forearms? For years people thought those spikes belonged on the end of Iguanodon's nose, making it look like a rhinoceros. Then scientists found whole Iguanodon skeletons and saw the spikes attached to the Iguanodon's hands.

Five Archaeopteryx gliding to a rock.

What a sight it would have been to see this primitive creature swoop down from the sky and land on a tree or rock. Because Archaeopteryx had feathers it is considered a bird, not a dinosaur. However, it did not have the necessary bone structure to flap its wings, so it could not fly. Still, with a good running start into the wind, it could certainly have become airborne.

Monoclonius
(Mah-no-CLO-nee-us)

Styracosaurus
(Sty-rack-o-SOAR-us)

Triceratops
(Tri-SAIR-o-tops)

Six Ceratopsians wearing frills and purple socks.

Ceratopsian is the group name for the horned dinosaurs. The number of horns varied, as did the size and shape of the frill around the Ceratopsian's head. Scientists speculate that the frill helped to guard the dinosaur s neck as well as to provide some muscular support for the animal's large head. Scissor-like teeth helped these herbivores, or plant-eaters, chew on tough leaves and ferns. They grazed in herds, much like cattle would graze in a field today.

Seven Plesiosaurus swimming in the seas.

Plesiosaurus was a marine reptile that lived at the same time as dinosaurs. Using its limbs as paddles, Plesiosaurus moved about freely in the water, probably dining on fish and other marine life. It is not known whether Plesiosaurus gave birth to live young, the way dolphins and whales do, or if it laid reptilian eggs on land.

Eight Brontosaurus browsing in the trees.

You could probably recognize this all-time favourite dinosaur in your sleep! Brontosaurus is the popular name for the dinosaur scientists call Apatosaurus (Uh-pat-o-SOAR-us). This huge plant-eater probably travelled in herds. Palaeontologists, scientists who study fossils, think the larger adults may have walked on the outside of the herd in order to protect their young from meat-eating dinosaurs.

Nine Ankylosaurus with armour on their backs.

This dinosaur had some of the best protection around. It had a hard, bony back like a turtle's, but it probably couldn't tuck its legs and head under its armour plating, the way a turtle can. Bony plates, spikes, and a heavy club tail made Ankylosaurus a tough opponent.

Corythosaurus
(Cor-ith-o-SOAR-us)

Lambeosaurus
(Lam-bee-o-SOAR-us)

Parasaurolophus
(Pair-a-soar-AWL-o-fuss)

Ten Hadrosaurids sporting funny hats.

"Duckbills" is the common, everyday name given to this wonderful-looking group of creatures. Even though their broad snouts looked "ducklike," Hadrosaurids lived on land, browsing on such vegetation as twigs, pine needles, and fruit. Many of these dinosaurs had crests on top of their heads. Different-shaped crests may have helped the various kinds of duckbills recognize each other during the mating season. Crests may also have aided the duckbills in calling to each other; the sound might have been amplified as it passed through the hollow tubes and spaces inside.